THE SONG IN THE SHADOW

A FORM BEFORE CONTENT. 9
THE SCREEN............ 14
INSIDE THE PAINTING.. 20
GAME ENVIRONMENT..... 29
MAKING SPACE......... 35
REPETITION........... 41
tHE TRANSFORMERS..... 53
INNUMERABLE THREADS.. 59

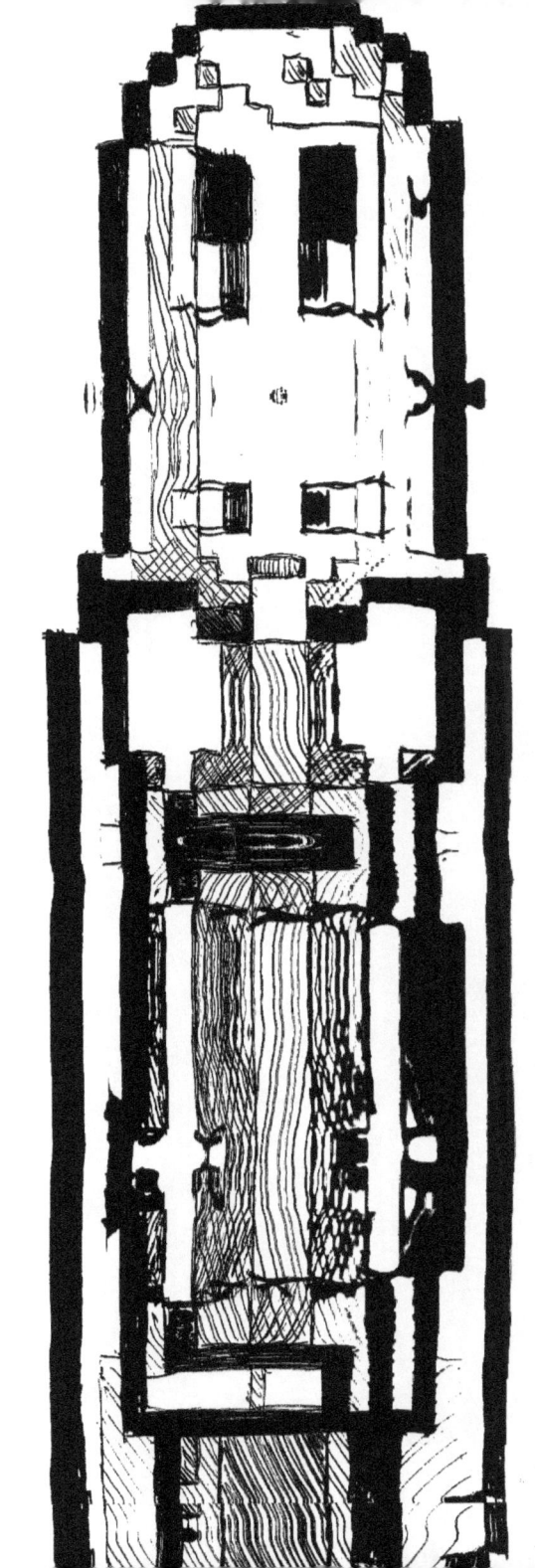

A FORM BEFORE CONTENT

   To make the book in reverse: begin with the design and the layout. Consider the size and weight of the book. How will the words be arranged on the pages? How dense will the text be? Proceed to the table of contents and write the chapter headings. Where will the blank pages be? Find words to fill all the remaining pages.
   To make the painting in reverse: begin with the complete image and slowly subtract from it. When there is enough room, begin to alternate the contents with whatever is around you. When the painting is full again, subtract more from it. Grab more stuff. How does it work when you put new things in there? Keep changing the parts until it functions according to its own logic.
   The whole has to presuppose the parts. To generate the work, one must reach beyond to the not-internal for

something that can serve the need at hand. Content comes from the unconscious. It is a virtual pouring forth of our hidden selves. The contents of the mind, whatever they may be, is what will fill in the gaps. If the mind is filled with theories, then theory will undoubtedly make its way forward. If the mind is full of clutter then the clutter will come out.

This pouring forth is a process of syntheses, of moving beyond that which can be controlled. Here, countless stories and thoughts reassemble themselves outside of reasonable reasoning.

Repressed thoughts also come out most strongly in this process. What is concealed can become obvious (or at least legible). This is why we are so averse to letting the unconscious work unfiltered—even when this may be the very thing that we want most to undertake.

As a strategy, a form before content is a matter of stepping aside and letting the creative process happen without judgement. On the surface this sounds simple, but we know that this is one of the hardest things imaginable to do. It involves trust in the unconscious: trust that it is not going to embarrass us; trust that it won't show off our flaws; but especially, trust that it won't show how out of control we really are when we are trying to maintain an illusion of being in control. This is the limit that we come up to when we begin with the whole and work backward to the particular.

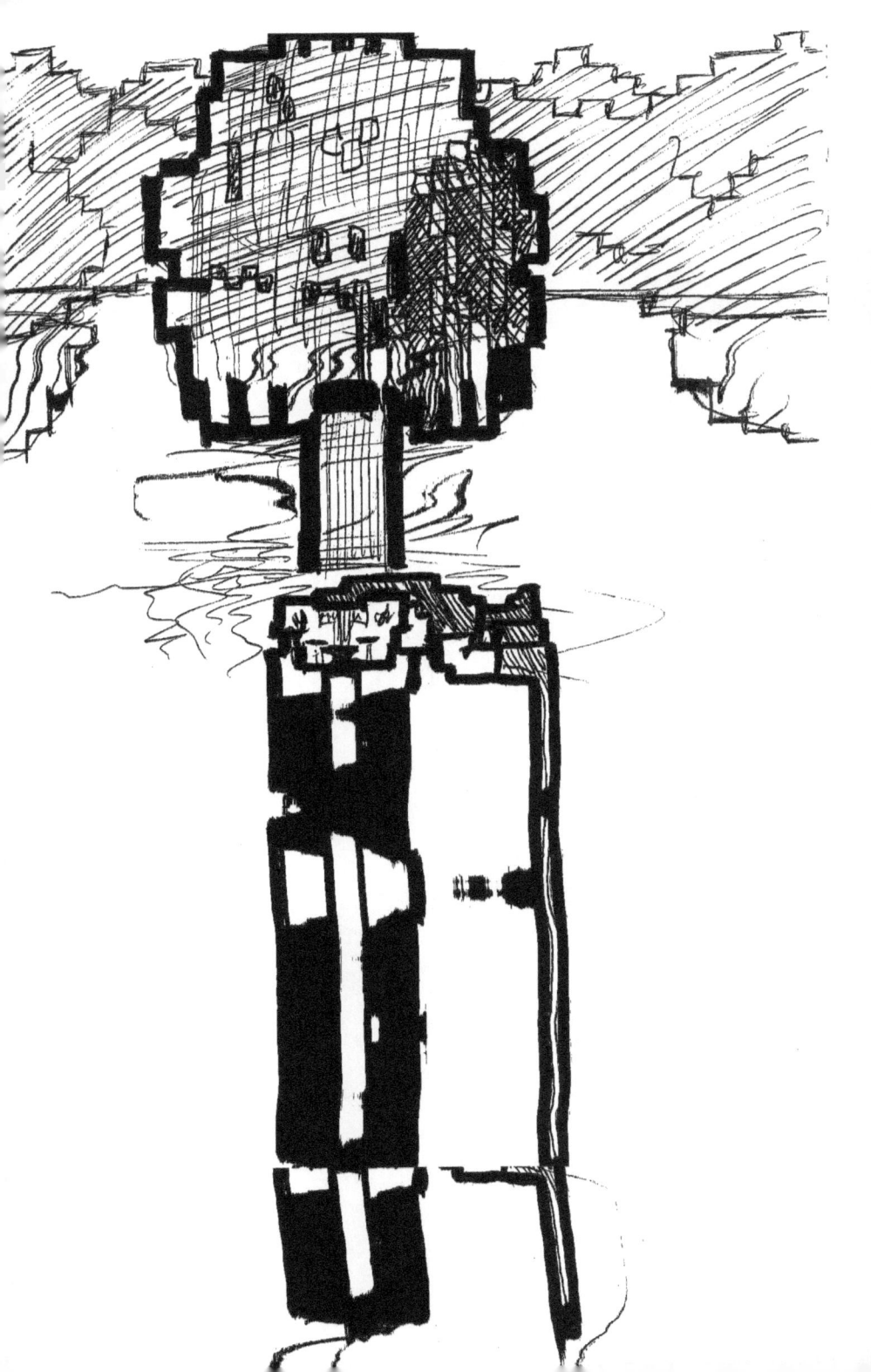

THE SCREEN

The first marks that are made on the surface are squeegee-like. White paint has been dragged across the plexiglass in long strokes. There are rhythms to this first layer, varying speeds, different intensities of motion and occasional stoppages. We see changes in direction and changes in the speed of the motion. It leaves a range of smears, clear and messy, across the underside of the plastic substrate.

Sometimes there is a fuck up; clearly a mistake that has had to be corrected—wiped away, washed off or repainted—then it was painted and scraped again. These mistakes leave their traces in the fold.

The scraping marks are made by dragging a slice of densely corrugated cardboard across the plastic. It is a finely rippled surface which leaves distinct patterns in the removal process. These hatch marks become grooves, like those of a record, tracing out a kind of sonic space.

The type of space traced is not uniform, it can at times be expansive and at others constricted. At some points it appears chaotic, while it is clearly delineated at others.

This web of lines is the screen; a grooved medium through which the viewer will look. It is an environment which connects, binds and submerges the imagery that will go underneath it into a tense unity. The screen sets the stage for activity yet to come. It generates the fold from which something will emerge. It is the field.

The squeegee as a painting tool is usually used as a way of affecting a pre-existent image or mark. The smear obscures the image, removes or transforms it. Richter's blur or

Bacon's smear are distortions of an earlier painted action. In my current work, there is a kinship to this idea of distortion through the smear, but it functions within a different causal relationship to the painted images. It anticipates rather than reacts. Movement presupposes content. Because the screen is painted first, it never follows the contours of the imagery underneath. It is separate from that which it mediates.

    The screen is also situated in an unusual space. It is internal to the painting—it is behind the plexiglass—but it is extraneous to the figures contained within. It both connects and distances these figures.

    We find that there are breaks in the screen, where parts of the original scraping have been razored away, and a new gesture has been inlaid into the void. These insertions are visible through changes in direction in the grains of the marks. Similar to joints in woodworking, where the grains of wood have shifted, this results in the surface having different densities. If this is a screen, it is one that appears to be often in need of repair.

The screen levels out the differences among the elements of the painting. It places them into a non-hierarchical arrangement and sews them into connections that are not usually possible. It turns a series of static images into a montage. It enables a transitional relationship between things which can become more than the sum of their parts. It is the glue of the assemblage; the noise that allows the figure to dismantle its own likeness.

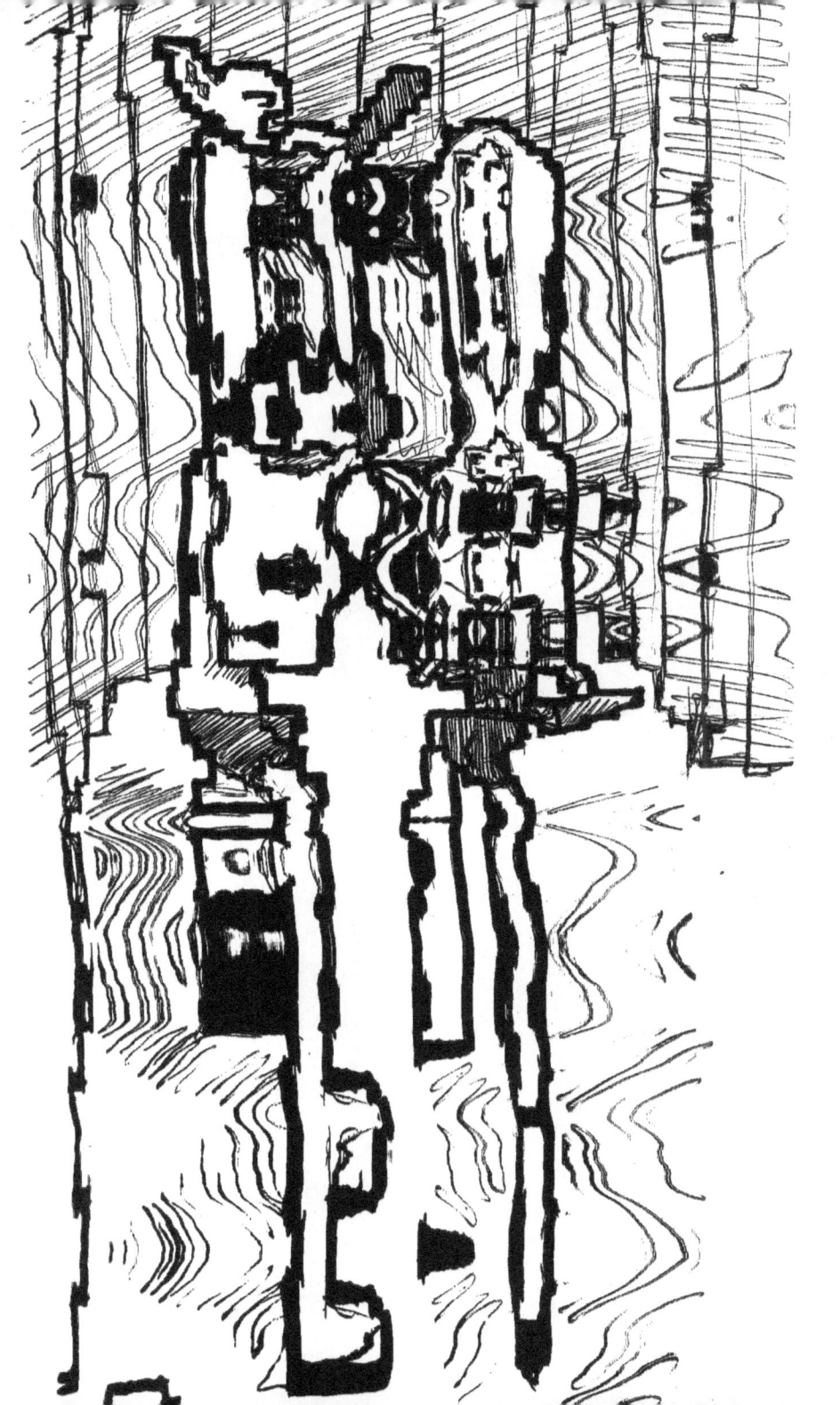

INSIDE THE PAINTING

Walter Benjamin proposed that while the painter is like the magician, who heals (creates) from the outside, by placing hands on the sick person, the filmmaker is more like a surgeon. The surgeon heals by cutting into the patient's body; working from within. The painter keeps a distance from reality, whereas the filmmaker cuts into and transforms the very reality itself (Benjamin 230).

Like the surgeon's procedure my paintings take place on the inside. I work not on the surface but on the back side; rather than building up, I build behind.

Everything is inverted in this operation. What you see is always the process backwards: the initial marks are in front and each subsequent layer is behind the first.

Effectively, I am inside the painting. It is as though I am filling up the window to the outside world. The more I paint, the more the interior void-space of the painting disappears. What begins as window, fills up more and more to the absolute flatness of the plexiglass.

The body is painted from within itself, but the body is also the site where transformations can occur.

Unlike the process of surface painting, here the painter-surgeon is able to perform the organ transplant, to transpose organic structures from one body to another.

In order to do this, sections are removed sliced away with a razor. This scraping back of the paint, all the way to the plexiglass, reveals an interior void once again. Other images can then be inserted, spliced into these gaps, again filling in the void. This method of combination is different from collage. Here the pieces are not organized one upon one another, but actually into one another.

Perhaps the painting is dying, and needs a new organ to enable it to survive. This involves the cutting, changing of organs and then the suturing of the wound.

In this analogy, images are bodies with the potential to fragment and reorganize within other bodies. The figures that are depicted in these arrangements

Like the filmmaker's production, in these works what we see is not reality represented but a new environment assembled out of pieces of other images. The montage is not mimetic, it is virtual. Similarly, my own paintings are generating new figurations and environments.

The first works in this new series have

all taken older failed works and used these as bodies to transplant into. These were paintings that had little hope of resolution. They had bodies which have already died or have little hope of recovery. They no longer functioned as living, breathing processes.

I sliced into these cadavers, opened up new space for other organs to be placed. This breathed new life into them. There is a kind of violence involved that could only work on a failed painting; on an abject body. The painting has to have reached a point where there is no hope, where there could be no mistake. The body has already died so there is no chance of further damage or loss. This hopelessness of the failed work is what allows the catastrophe to work its magic.

This necromantic salvage operation is a kind of monstrous assemblage according to the logic of the rhizome. I am looking for the Frankenstein: the arrangement of interior elements that function as a whole.

Although chance is important in the process, the search for a Frankenstein is not a random operation. It is guided by a virtual form; a vision of the whole that can be grasped in advance. This whole is only comprehensible in its form not in its composition.

How does one work towards a form without the content to fill it in? We proceed towards the virtual form through action rather than concept. The guiding methodology is that of Intuition.

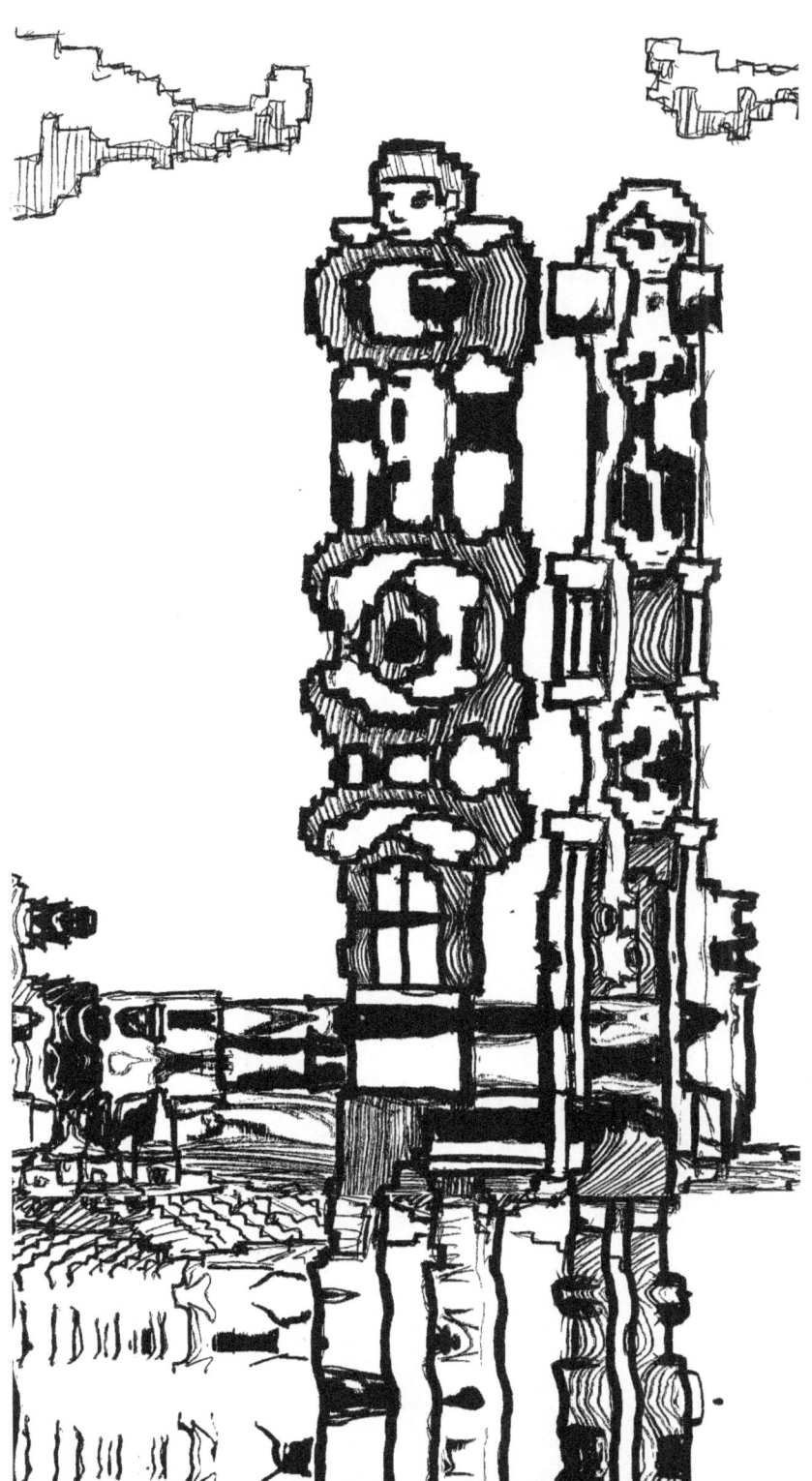

GAME ENVIRONMENT

"Art, like games, is a translation of experience. What we have already felt or seen in one situation we are suddenly given a new kind of material. (McLuhan 460)"

Over the past several years, I've been designing my own videogame. The game is based on the aesthetics and style of games that were popular in my adolescence. These 1980's role playing games were fantasy and sci-fi adventures that took place over sprawling maps. They had pixelated characters, monsters and terrain.

My game recreates the style of this era, and develops a new storyline, cast of characters and a variety of graphics.

For most of the time I was working on this game, I considered it something separate from my art practice and did not explore it as a potential source. I've intuitively known that there was something important there to be explored, but hadn't seen how to bring it into the fold of my art practice.

As I've engaged in the chimeric, surgical operation that I've been describing in this paper, I've been incorporating imagery from my game into the paintings.

The game lends a much different aesthetic to the work, a distinctly retro vibe. It brings in narrative elements, putting plot devices onto the painted stage to be transformed in new contexts.

They also allow for a different logic to drive the process. The game itself is dictating the parameters for the production of the content (the graphics). The graphics are then adapted to the painting. This allows for a kind of self-organizing of the systems that are conjoining and affecting one another.

Game environment is a strange space; we enter into places where there is no space. Making the game is an even stranger experience, because it is possible to alternate between making a space and enter into it. From inside the game I can move to the outside, change the space and then enter into it again. This ability to move in and out of the game, which also moves in and out of the painting is a pleasant kind of recursion to me.

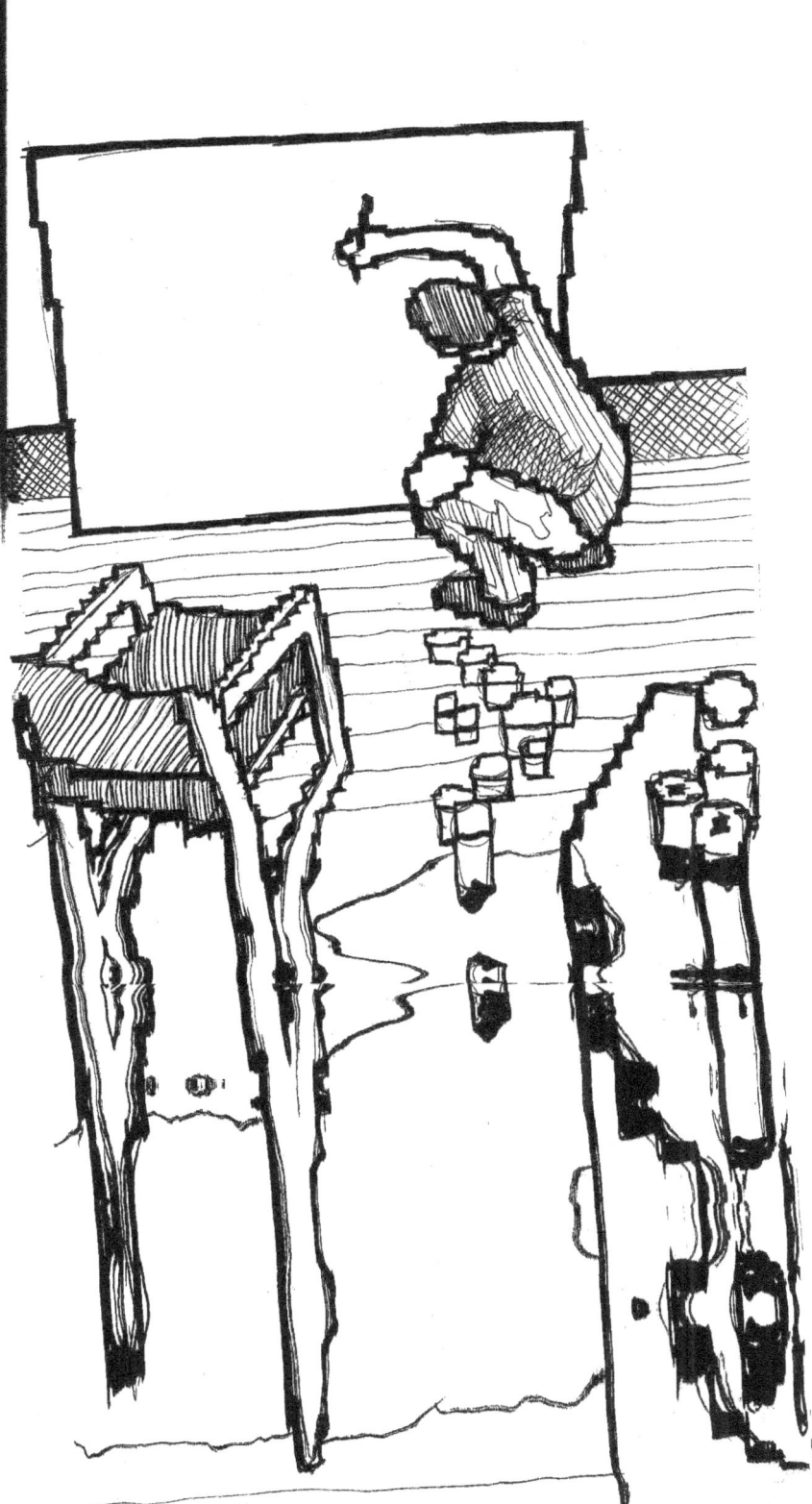

MAKING SPACE

Deleuze famously said that the canvas is already full even before the painter makes a single mark. While it may seem like the possibilities for the blank canvas are endless, one must continually come up against cliché: How does one say anything new? How can we not repeat the same stories that have been told over and over again? (Deleuze &1) Approaching this fullness—looking for a way to make space—is what every painter is doing; we each have to find our own way around this situation.

In my practice over the past few years, I've made a ton of works but haven't felt that what I was doing was really the work. I was always busy, able to make pieces all the time; but the pieces felt like studies of some kind; like parts of work rather than complete in themselves.

The theory that I was working with was one of switching tasks. I had found in the past that having more than one body of work going at a time was a good way to stay active in the studio. When series A gets to be a chore it is nice to have series B to switch to. Changing modes of working keeps up the momentum; allows you to overcome stagnation.

This strategy worked well for me, so I built on it: expanded it into many series. If two series work well, why not work on five? I began to explore more and more threads. Every tangent was possibly a new seires... and I was always moving, always painting.

Looking back now, I see that this constant expansion was in fact closing off space. What I needed was to make space:

to pause.

Once I stopped the activity, then suddenly I could see and hear all sorts of possibilities in the work that I was tuning out before. Abruptly I decided that I could make space in my paintings for my game imagery. I cut into them and found a place.

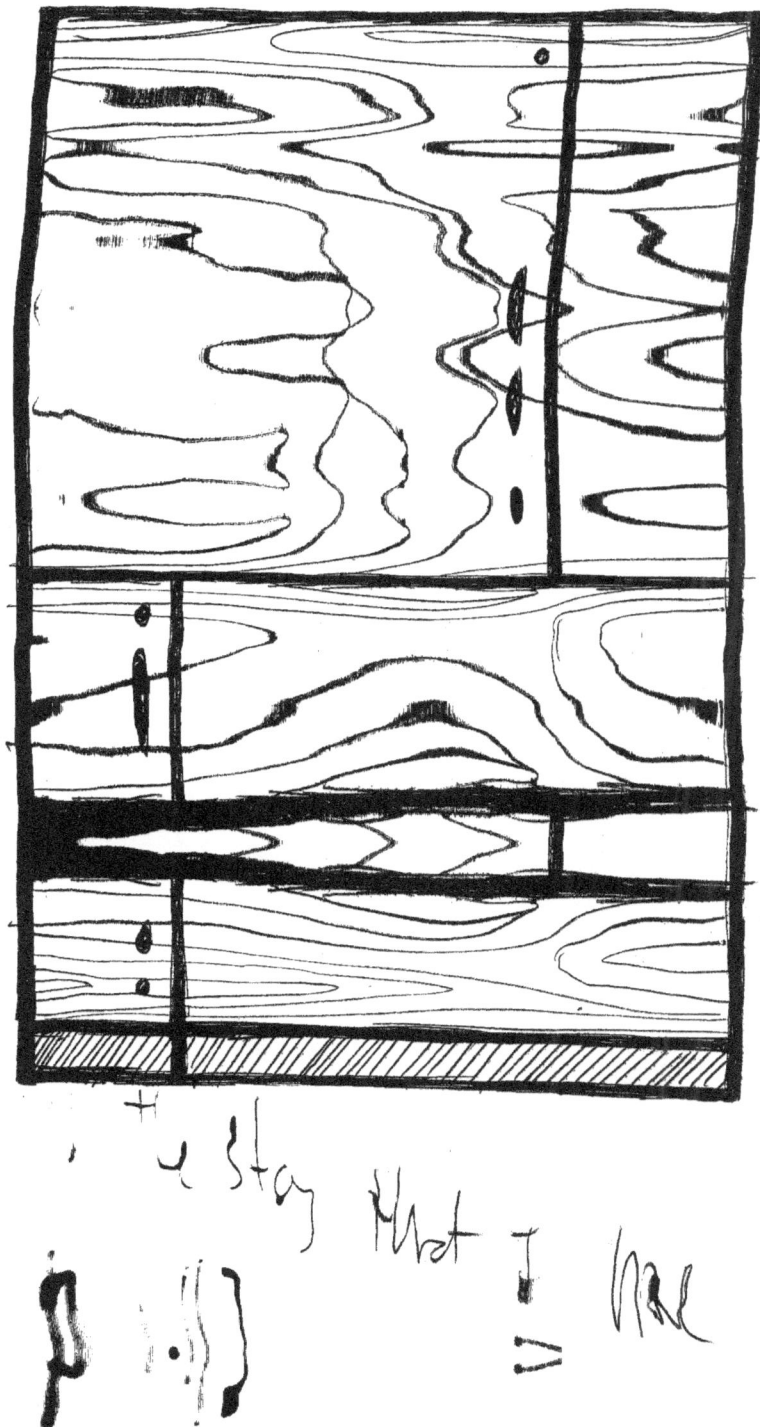

REPETITION

"We are right when we say that habit is formed by the repetition of an effort; but what would be the use of repeating it, if the result were always to reproduce the same thing? The true effect of repetition is to decompose and then to recompose, and thus appeal to the intelligence of the body. (Bergson 111)"

Emulation has always been one of the painter's' primary methods of learning: the student recreates the masterwork in order to learn certain techniques that can only be learned in this way.

In art school, when becoming familiar with the codes of the contemporary and the avant-garde, learning also proceeds by emulation. We repeat the gestures of the ready-made and the assemblage; we test the different approaches to representation and abstraction; we experiment with the various phases of art history that we are most drawn to.

If the goal is to advance to an original method—an original stylistic process—we must first emulate: break down the process into its constituent parts. This breaking down isn't just a conceptual operation; if it were, learning the art of painting would be simply a matter of studying its history.

To emulate is to encode the process in the body; to know it from within. To really engage in the act, we must first commit to the body a series of actions that we already visualized in the mind.

Bergson explains that our knowing an action conceptually is nothing like being able to perform it. The idea of an action is a diagram; an impression of the whole without any parts. We might be able to picture the action of playing a piano sonata. We can imagine the way the player moves, how she is positioned in relation to her instrument, and recognize when it is not being done correctly, but to carry out the action requires a much different type of training than simply picturing the action.

"This is because the diagram… indicates only its salient outlines… but to be able to carry it out, we must have also brought our body to understand it. Now the logic of the body admits of no tacit implications. It demands that all the constituent parts of the required movement shall be set forth one by one, and then put back together again. Here a complete analysis is necessary, in which no detail is neglected, and an actual synthesis, in which nothing is curtailed (112)"

To become skillful, we must repeat. With

painting, one of the things that we learn as we proceed to greater levels of familiarity with the medium, is that you proceed by taking suggestions from the material. There is a definite playfulness or openness that has to be in the work—a willingness to see the possibility of the material as it is unfolding on the surface.

    Proceeding by suggestion is allowing the material to participate in the finding of the likeness. This is also the happy accident, the smear or smudge that actually looks more natural than the mark that would have otherwise been.

    For some painters, the accident is more prominent than others. When we work through intuition—with the accident/the catastrophe as method—we can sometimes stumble upon a thing that is much greater than what we are usually capable of producing according to that which we have mastered.

This is what I see in the work of Francis Bacon, whose work, in particular over the first ten years of his practice, was often repetitious within the various phases of his oeuvre.

His early masterpiece, *Three Studies for Figures at the Base of a Crucifixion*, 1944, has a quality that he continuously described in his interviews: the ability to speak beyond himself—beyond his own *abilities*—to unlock the unconscious and to trap unexpected layers of sensation that are normally inaccessible. *Three Studies* was such a remarkable success for Bacon that it seems to have had continual pull for him for the rest of his life. My proposal is that he continuously returned to different aspects in the *Three Studies* to try to understand how and why they came together so perfectly.

His practice, for the decade following the creation of this work, revolved around a dissection of the various aspects of the painting in turn, identifying, isolating and understanding how each aspect functions, before being able to use all of these elements masterfully in the later stages of his career.

Bacon said that the three studies was a fluke – that everything just happened to gel in a certain way that he wasn't able to understand or capture again in the following years. What I observed, looking through his paintings piece by piece, is that he worked in many series (often calling them studies), each of which takes on a specific attribute that can be found in the *Three Studies*. He isolated one aspect of the work— for instance: the scream more than the horror; the accident incorporated in the portrait; the caged head; the religious icon as horrific.

What we see in Bacon's trajectory after the Three Studies is that there is a difference between knowing the art conceptually and knowing it through the body. Bacon did not produce another work that accessed all of these attributes of interest until he had broken them down into their constituent parts and trained his (painterly) body to be able to access each of these aspects, to be able to do them rather than think them.

After this period of fragmentation, Bacon was then able to combine all of the attributes and to make complex work which defied simple explanation.

To make the work he had to commit each of the elements to immediate knowledge; to the intuitive embodied knowing.

In my own practice, I similarly have employed a

fragmentation of the whole, tangential development, and re-assembling into a new configuration. The hope is that such a process can lead to an understanding through the body, in a similar way to what Bacon has achieved.

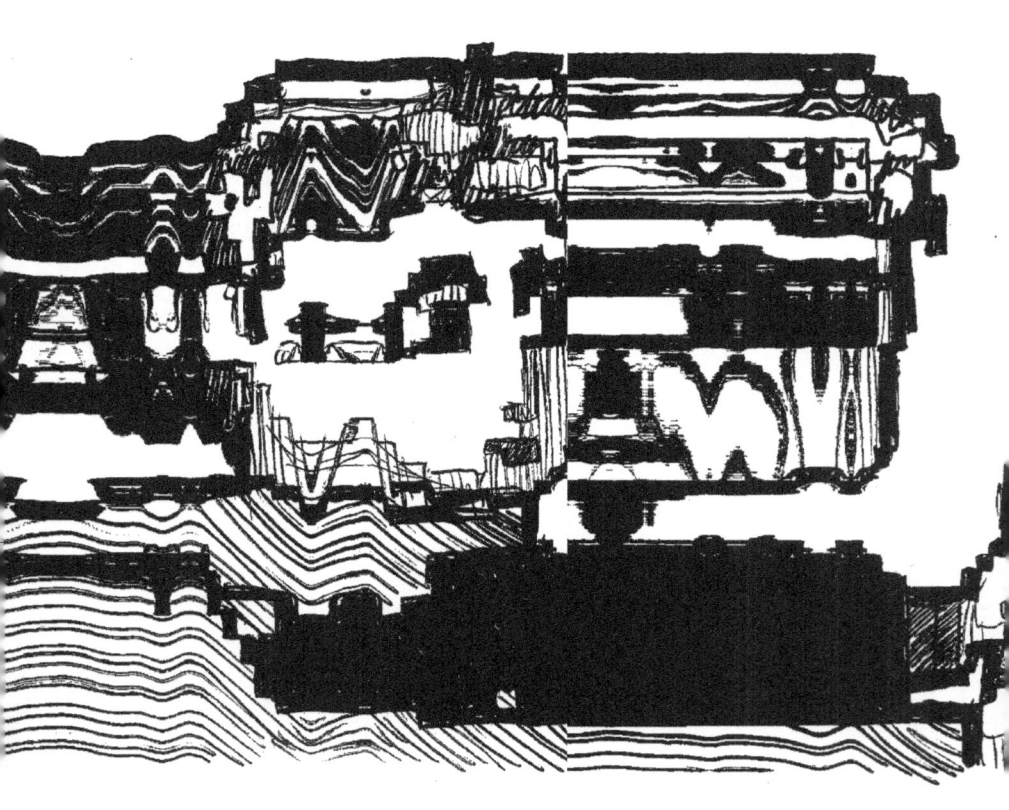

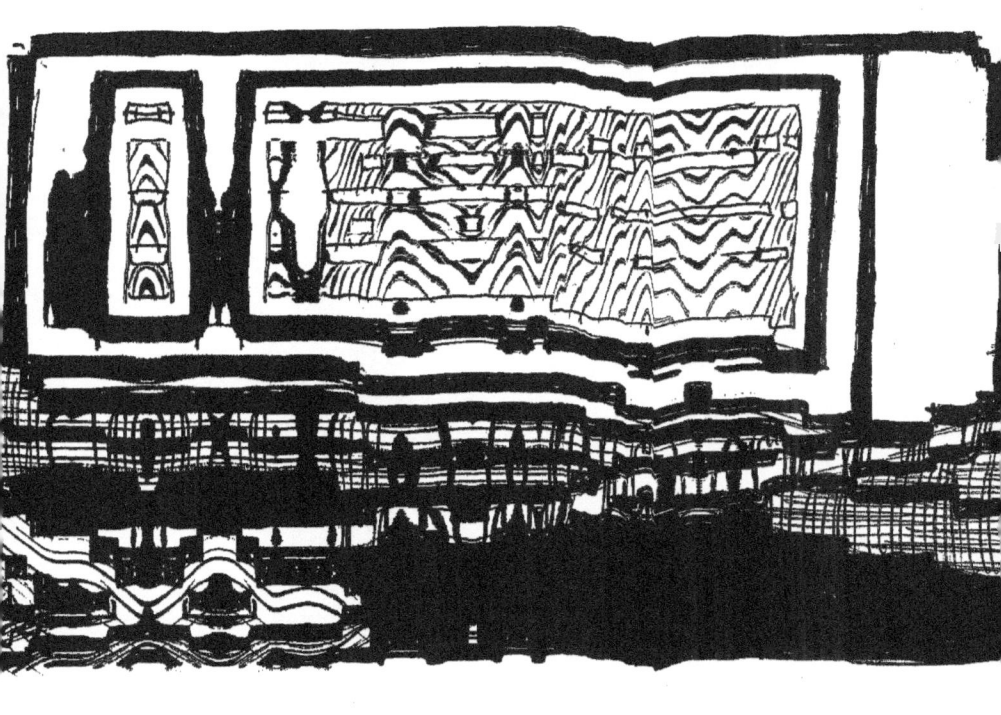

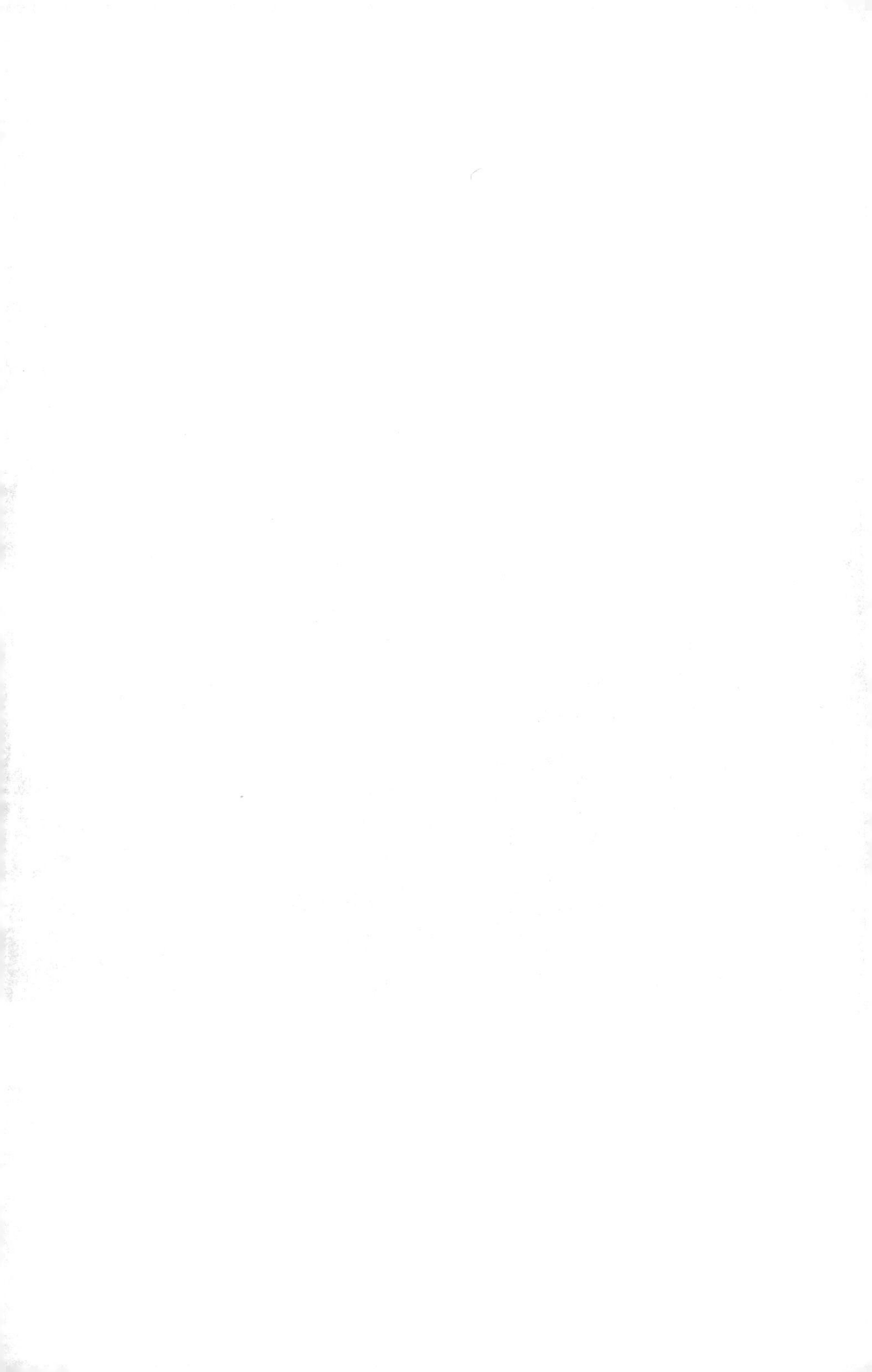

THE TRANSFORMERS

In the mid-1980's there was a line of toys made by Hasbro called the transformers. Each toy had two (or more) forms that it could take: 1. a recognizable vehicle, object or animal; and 2. a robot (or rather a clichéd version of what a robot might look like: a boxy, mechanical kind of figure).

The toys themselves were beautiful objects, expertly designed with material awareness and sophisticated colour schemes (they utilized intense Van Gogh-esque colouration, often through analogous and split-complementary colour schemes).

They were also exceptionally well marketed, being integrated with a cartoon series which had a compelling story that added depth to these objects that child consumers could collect and enjoy.

The toys therefore were almost magically

endowed. The Transformers became myth. Not only were they ritualistic objects, allowing the stories to be enacted as rites; but they were also avatars to the cartoon.

Although recognizable in either of their configurations, there are always visible echoes of the alternate arrangements within the current form. The robot form has automobile parts sticking out of its body, the vehicle is broken up by lines all over its surface (which allow it to transform).

They are never static. They are always charged with the potential to take another form. They were always kinetic, able to be two things at once.

Transformers have the ability to fragment and to rearrange their elements into a new, distinct arrangement. The two forms are both wholes, with their own internal logic, but influenced by, and with clues to, their alternate function mixed in. Like the chimera, they are hybrid creatures. They are mythical monsters, gods or demigods.

    The Transformer binds together myth and the assemblage into a neat consumable object. Now that these objects are rare and hard to find, they are the perfect treasure for nostalgic Ebay shoppers, seeking to reconnect with their lost sense of a magical world.

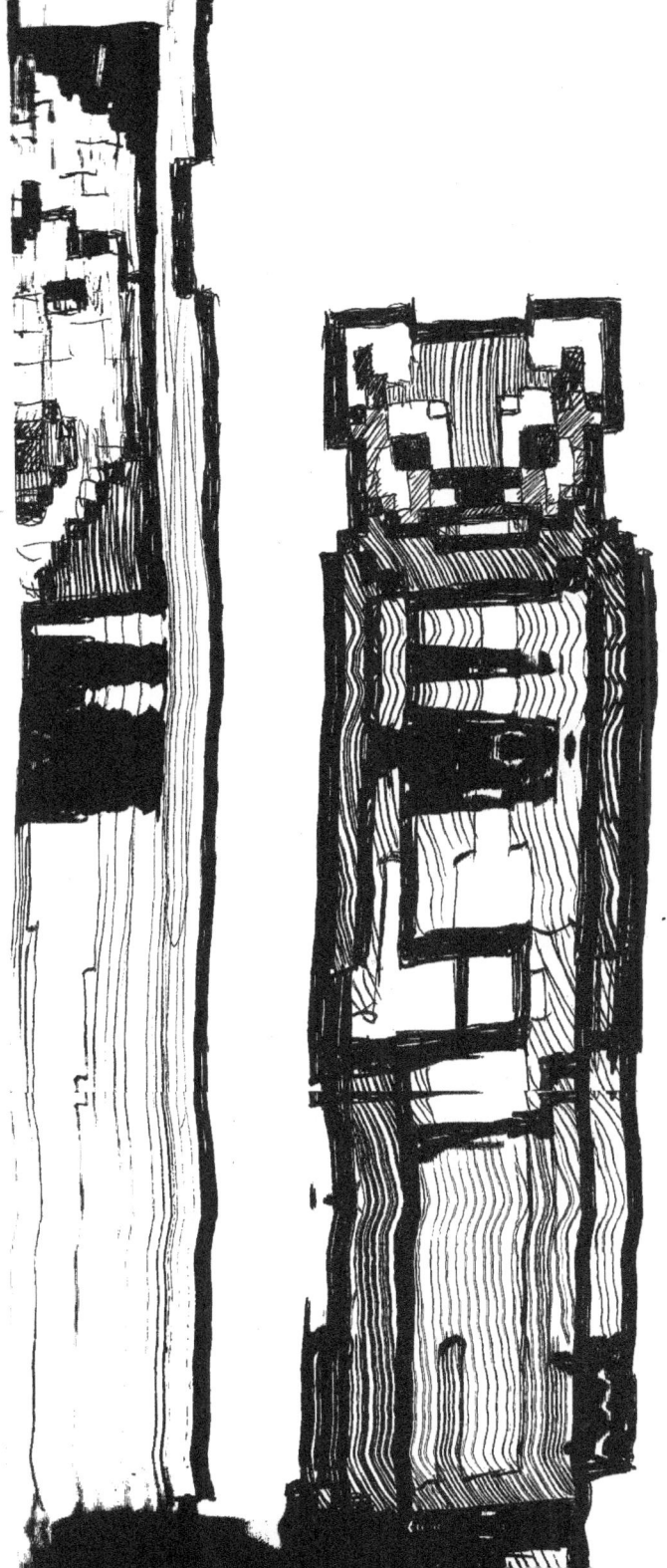

INNUMERABLE THREADS

There are countless ways that we can approach the work; countless stories we could tell to explain it, describe it or utilize it. But, though we may try to get closer and closer to it, we find that everything we say can only access a part of it—can only articulate particular qualities—never the whole of the work itself. The things that we say never quite get to the center of the work. There is always something important, something essential that is left out.

Wholeness

Bergson explains that we don't understand things through their parts and then move up to wholes, but rather we always begin with the whole and work backwards to the parts.

Take for example the experience of having an afterimage. Look at the

59

face of someone you have never seen before and then abruptly look away. You will still be able to see them momentarily as an afterimage (Bergson MM 102).

This likeness that you recall is not a group of fragmented, partial features that were individually perceived. Rather, what you see is an impression of a whole; a likeness that is unified though difficult to hold in conscious awareness. If you try to describe the details, you will find that you cannot; you understand the afterimage in its completeness, but are unable to retrace the parts in their specific details. If, for instance, you were to try to record the face by drawing it out on paper, you would discover that you do not understand the image well enough at all, even though you have a sense of being able to recall the likeness of that person.

Describing the work is like describing the afterimage: it was completely known in the moment, but recreating it outside of the event is impossible. This is because what is being described is not a concept, it is an environment, and the only way to know an environment is to be in the centre of it; to be on the inside looking out.

Being in the centre of the work is to be present with it; to experience it through sensation and sense rather than as a rational narrative. It is necessarily non-linguistic. It is to merge with the work, where the distinction between self and other fade away. When the illusion of separateness dissolves there is only the painting-as-a-verb; the becoming painting.

Threads can certainly be identified within the whole, but they must not be mistake for the work itself. Threads are just threads. Like comparing sketches of a street in Paris to the actual street; no amount of sketches will ever recreate the actual experience of that real environment (Bergson).

Threads can be pathways but they can become barriers. What is said about the work can change the terrain, can modify the flows in those regions and can establish boundaries. These are problems of territorialisation.

Whenever a practice is enclosed it is in danger of stagnating, of losing the ability to flow as an ever-changing event.

The difficulty is in finding the threads which can be used as pathways back to the centre rather than being barriers. Undoubtedly such pathways exist, but the only way to know where they lead is to test them. I am writing about the work as though throwing dust at an invisible form.

How does one talk about the work without moving too far outside the work? How to define the parameters without causing it to stagnate? These are the concerns that I struggle with, as I have a tendency to get caught in the trap of over-analyzing and reducing wholes down to concepts and strategies. I'm looking to find threads, stories really, that might be told about the work which don't limit it. It is a search for a way to come closer and closer the centre of the work itself.

Towards this end, I have tried to approach this text as a series of spaces—as textual environments—that might be entered into to find the way back to the centre.

Works Cited

Benjamin, W. *Illuminations: Essays and Reflections* (New York, Schocken Books 1969)

Bergson, H. *Matter and Memory* Trans. N. Paul and W. Palmer (New York: Zone Books, (1896) 1991).

Bergson, H. *The Creative Mind: An Introduction to Metaphysics* (New York, Dover, 2007).

Deleuze, G. *Francis Bacon: The Logic of Sensation* (Minneapolis: University of Minnesota Press, 2002).

Deleuze, G. and Felix Guattari. *A Thousand Plateaus: Capitalism and Schizophrenia* (London, Penguin Classics, (1980) 2009)

McLuhan, Marshall. *The Book of Probes*. Corte Madera: Ginko Press, 2003.

Works Referenced:

Carson, Anne. *Float*. (Lancaster: McClelland and Stewart, 2016).

Csikszentmihalyi, M. *Flow: The Psychology of Optimal Experience*. (New York: Harper & Row, 1990)

Delanda, M. *A Thousand Years of Nonlinear History* (Zone, New York, 2000).

Delanda, M. *Assemblage Theory* (Edinburgh, Edinburgh University Press, 2016).

Deleuze, G. and Felix Guattari. *What is Philosophy?* (New York, Columbia University Press, 1996)

Deleuze, G. and Felix Guattari. *Anti-Oedipus: Capitalism and Schizophrenia* (London, Penguin Classics, 2009)

Grosz, E. (ed.) *Becomings: Explorations in Time, Memory and Futures* (Ithica,

Cornell University Press, 1999).

Grosz, E. *The Nick of Time: Politics, Evolution, and the Untimely* (Durham, Duke, 2004).

Guerlac, S. *Thinking in Time: An Introduction to Henri Bergson* (Ithica, Cornell University Press, 2006).

Johnstone, K. *Impro: Improvisation and the Theatre* (London, Routledge 2012)

Jung, K. *Dreams*. (Princeton, Princeton University Press, 1974).

Levi-Strauss, C. *Structural Anthropology* (New York, Basic Books, 1963).

Levi-Strauss, C. *The Savage Mind* (Chicago, University of Chicago Press, 1969).

Marks, L. "A Noisy Brush with the Infinite," in *The Oxford Handbook of*

Sound and Image in Digital Media (New York, Oxford University Press, 2013).

Nietzsche, F. *On the Genealogy of Morals* (New York, Doubleday, 1956)

Schafer, R. M. *The Tuning of the World.* (New York, Alfred A. Knopf, 1977).

Sylvester, D. *Interviews with Francis Bacon 1962-1979.* (Alden Press, 1975).

Winnicott, D. *Playing and Reality* (London, New York, Routledge, 2005)

Write, J. *The Philosopher's "I": Autobiography and the Search for the Self* (Albany, State University of New York Press, 2006).

www.ingramcontent.com/pod-product-compliance
Lightning Source LLC
Chambersburg PA
CBHW021507210526
45463CB00002B/925